Berklee
In the Pocket

Essential
Songwriter

Jimmy Kachulis
Jonathan Feist

Berklee Media

Vice President: Dave Kusek
Dean of Continuing Education: Debbie Cavalier
Business Manager: Linda Chady Chase
Technology Manager: Mike Serio
Marketing Manager, Berkleemusic: Barry Kelly
Senior Graphic Designer: David Ehlers

Berklee Press

Senior Writer/Editor: Jonathan Feist
Writer/Editor: Susan Gedutis Lindsay
Production Manager: Shawn Girsberger
Marketing Manager, Berklee Press: Jennifer Rassler
Product Marketing Manager: David Goldberg

ISBN 978-0-87639-054-2

1140 Boylston Street
Boston, MA 02215-3693 USA
(617) 747-2146

Visit Berklee Press Online at
www.berkleepress.com

DISTRIBUTED BY

HAL•LEONARD®
CORPORATION
7777 W. BLUEMOUND RD. P.O. BOX 13819
MILWAUKEE, WISCONSIN 53213

Visit Hal Leonard Online at
www.halleonard.com

Printed in the United States of America by Patterson Printing

11 10 09 08 07 06 05 04   5 4 3 2 1

Contents

Foreword

This book is based on the research and experience of hit-songwriter/ethnomusicologist Jimmy Kachulis, crafted into this handy pocket guide by writer/editor Jonathan Feist. These ideas and many other songwriting concepts are developed and illustrated in Jimmy's book series and online courses, *The Songwriter's Workshop.* The books and courses include workshops and recorded examples so that you can hear these tools in action. But this guide will serve you as a quick reference, to keep in your gig bag or next to your computer, for whenever writer's block strikes and you need some ideas.

The tools in this book have been used to create countless hit songs. The tools are a concise distillation of many years of research, chart-watching, and songwriting, and of countless longer books, classes, seminars, interactions with thousands of student songwriters, and of course, songs.

Part I presents charts that show chords based on each scale degree. Following each chart are common "power progressions" in each type of scale: major, minor, Mixolydian, Dorian, and blues.

To use them, choose a chord progression—for example, I(Maj7) IVMaj7 in major. Then choose a key for your song, and find the chords on the chart. (Numbers in parentheses indicate optional additional notes.) In the key of E, you'd play E(Maj7) AMaj7. A few hit songs are listed next to the power progression that they are based on. There are many, many more examples for each progression, and in many other styles.

Part II lists fifty-three ideas for how to customize each progression, adapting it to best support your own unique lyrics. For example, if the idea suggests changing the harmonic rhythm, you might play EMaj7 for three measures, and then AMaj7 for one measure. These tips are discussed in greater depth, and with recorded examples, in Jimmy Kachulis's *The Songwriter's Workshop* series, from Berklee Press.

Part III describes the most common forms and structures used in hit songs.

Part IV presents a sample songwriting process, to help you develop a productive working method, and keep your pen moving, should writer's block strike.

And part V presents the contact information for some of the most useful organizations in the. music industry.

Try many different possibilities, and follow whatever progressions, ideas, and working methods inspire you and keep you productive.

The only real rule of songwriting is to use whatever approach works best for you. We hope you find these materials to be helpful.

David Kusek
Vice President, Berklee Media

1. Power Progressions

Most hit songs are based on one of the following chord progressions. These progressions have a natural balance and gravity to them. They make songs feel soundly crafted, and create a sense of inevitability—that they are the "right" way for the chords to follow each other, and for the songs to progress. We call them *power progressions* because they do have power. They have been at the heart of countless songs, in all different styles of music, across many cultures and musical eras. These are the essential chord progressions that have rocked the world for as long as music has been based on harmony.

By customizing these progressions to different keys, grooves, harmonic rhythms, and other variations mentioned in part II of this handbook, you can use them to create an infinite number of songs.

Each key color has its own power progressions. To use one of these progressions in your songwriting, choose the one that seems to best suit your lyrics or melody, and then apply it to a key. Charts are shown with each type of key, indicating which chords go with which scale degrees, so you can use these progressions in any key. The triads are the essential chords; sevenths, indicated in parentheses, can be added, for extra color. The charts include suggested fretboard diagrams for guitarists and notated seventh chords for keyboard players.

The actual voicing you choose will depend on the progression, your melody, and your lyric story.

Once you have a progression and a key, groove on them, and use the ideas throughout this book to customize the progression to your lyrics. Power progressions are just the starting point for your grooves. Use your imagination to grow them into something unique.

Major

Major Chords

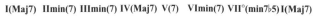

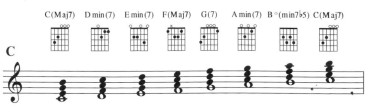

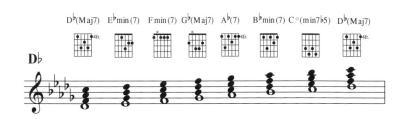

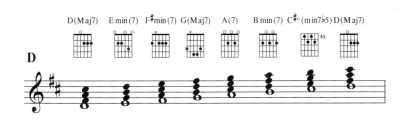

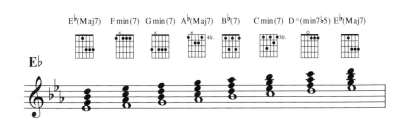

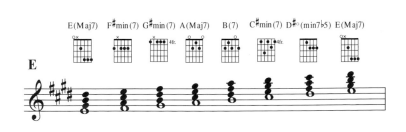

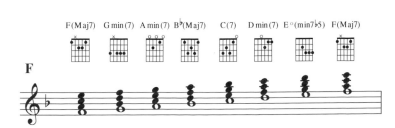

I(Maj7) IImin(7) IIImin(7) IV(Maj7) V(7) VImin(7) VII°(min7♭5) I(Maj7)

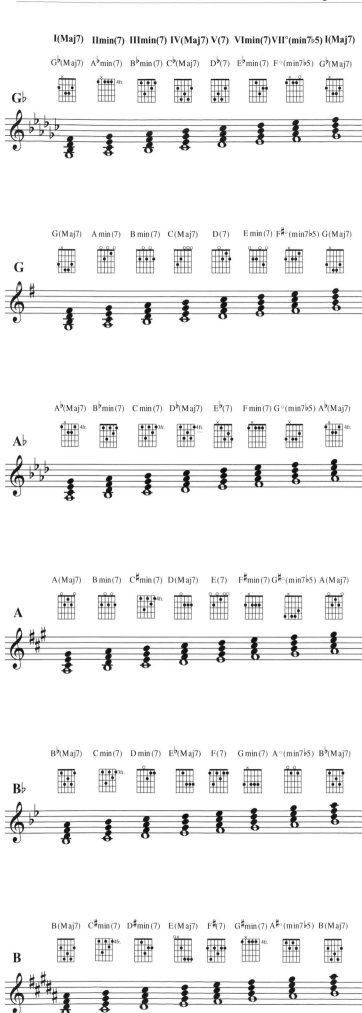

Major Power Progressions

These progressions are based on the *major scale.*

I   IV
C   F

"Just the Way You Are" [D], "Endless Love" [Bb],
"I Want to Hold Your Hand" [G],
"Help Me Make It through the Night" [C],
"Gone Country" [C]

I   IV   V
C   F   G

"Like a Rolling Stone" [C], "Twist and Shout" [F],
"River of Dreams" [G], "I Love Rock and Roll" [E],
"Here Comes the Sun" [A],
"Tonight I Celebrate My Love" [Eb],
"Tracks of My Tears" [G]

I   VImin   IImin   V
C   Amin   Dmin   G

Common variations:

I   IImin   VImin   IV   V
C   Dmin   Amin   F   G

IIImin   VImin   IImin   V
Emin   Amin   Dmin   G

"Savin' All My Love for You" [A], "Earth Angel" [Eb],
"This Boy" [D], "I'll Make Love to You" [D],
"Please Mister Postman" [A],
"If You Really Love Me" [C], "Breezin'" [D],
"In the Still of the Night" [C]

I   IImin   IIImin   IV
C   Dmin   Emin   F

"Here There and Everywhere" [G], "Longer" [G],
"Lean on Me" [C]

I   V/7   VImin   I/5   IV   I/3   IImin   V
C   G/B   Amin   C/G   F   C/E   Dmin   G

"Piano Man" [C], "Mr. Bojangles" [D],
"Man in the Mirror" [G]

8

Minor

Minor Chords

Note that V(7) is often substituted for the Vmin(7).

Imin(7) II°(min7♭5) ♭III(Maj7) IVmin(7) Vmin(7) ♭VI(Maj7) ♭VII(7) Imin(7) V(7)

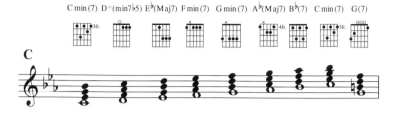

C min(7)   D°(min7♭5)   E♭(Maj7)   F min(7)   G min(7)   A♭(Maj7)   B♭(7)   C min(7)   G(7)

C

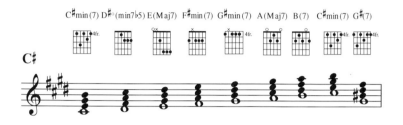

C♯min(7)   D♯°(min7♭5)   E(Maj7)   F♯min(7)   G♯min(7)   A(Maj7)   B(7)   C♯min(7)   G♯(7)

C♯

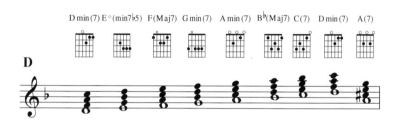

D min(7)   E°(min7♭5)   F(Maj7)   G min(7)   A min(7)   B♭(Maj7)   C(7)   D min(7)   A(7)

D

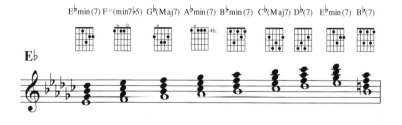

E♭min(7)   F°(min7♭5)   G♭(Maj7)   A♭min(7)   B♭min(7)   C♭(Maj7)   D♭(7)   E♭min(7)   B♭(7)

E♭

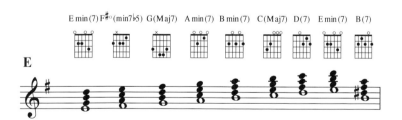

E min(7)   F♯°(min7♭5)   G(Maj7)   A min(7)   B min(7)   C(Maj7)   D(7)   E min(7)   B(7)

E

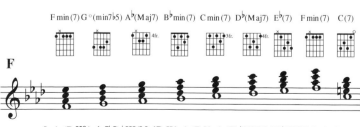

F min(7)   G°(min7♭5)   A♭(Maj7)   B♭min(7)   C min(7)   D♭(Maj7)   E♭(7)   F min(7)   C(7)

F

Imin(7) II°(min7♭5) ♭III(Maj7) IVmin(7) Vmin(7) ♭VI(Maj7) ♭VII(7) Imin(7) V(7)

9

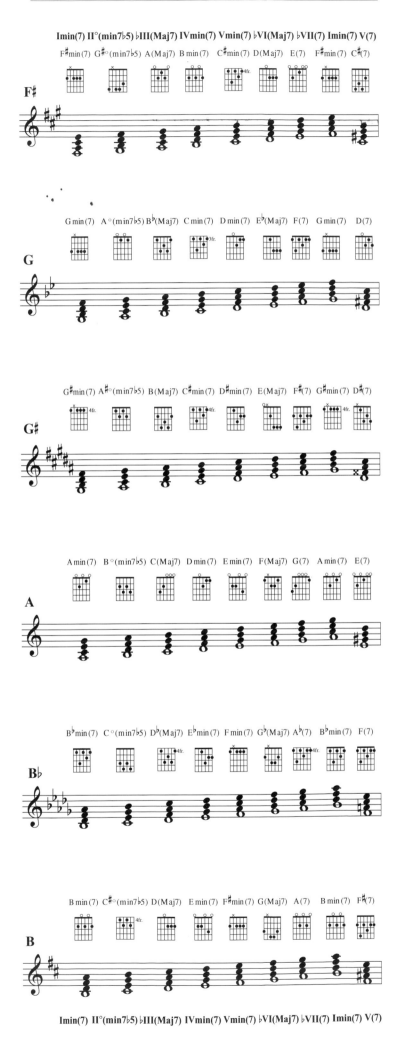

Minor Progressions

These progressions are based on the natural *minor scale.*

Imin   ♭**VII**
Cmin   B♭

"King of Pain" [Bmin], "Walking on the Moon" [Dmin], "We Are the Champions" [Cmin], "Ohio" [Amin], "Where Have All the Cowboys Gone?" [F♯min], "Wrapped Around Your Finger" [Amin]

Imin   ♭**VII**   ♭**VI**   ♭**VII**
Cmin   B♭   A♭   B♭

Common Variation:

Imin   ♭**VII**   ♭**VI**   **V**
Cmin   B♭   A♭   G

"All Along the Watchtower" [Amin], "Wrapped Around Your Finger" [Amin], "Standin' in the Shadows of Love" [Amin], "Remember (Walking in the Sand)" [Cmin], "Happy Together" [Emin], "Love Child" [B♭min]

Imin   **Vmin**
Cmin   Gmin

"Things We Said Today" [Gmin], "Where Have All the Cowboys Gone?" [F♯min]

Imin   **IVmin**
Cmin   Fmin

"I Shot the Sheriff" [Gmin], "Another One Bites the Dust" [Amin], "Boogie Wonderland" [Dmin]

11

Mixolydian

Mixolydian Chords

I(7)   IImin(7) III°(min7♭5) IV(Maj7) Vmin(7) VImin(7) ♭VII(Maj7) I(7)

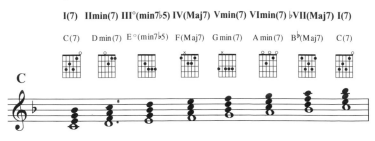

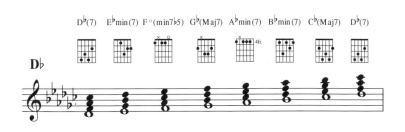

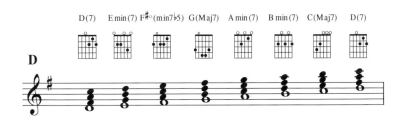

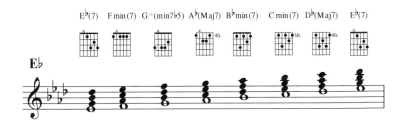

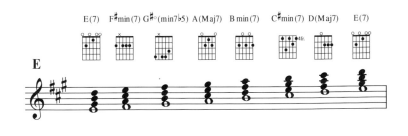

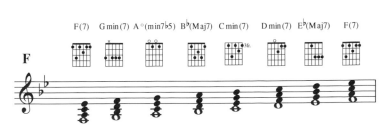

I(7) IImin(7) III°(min7♭5) IV(Maj7) Vmin(7) VImin(7) ♭VII(Maj7) I(7)

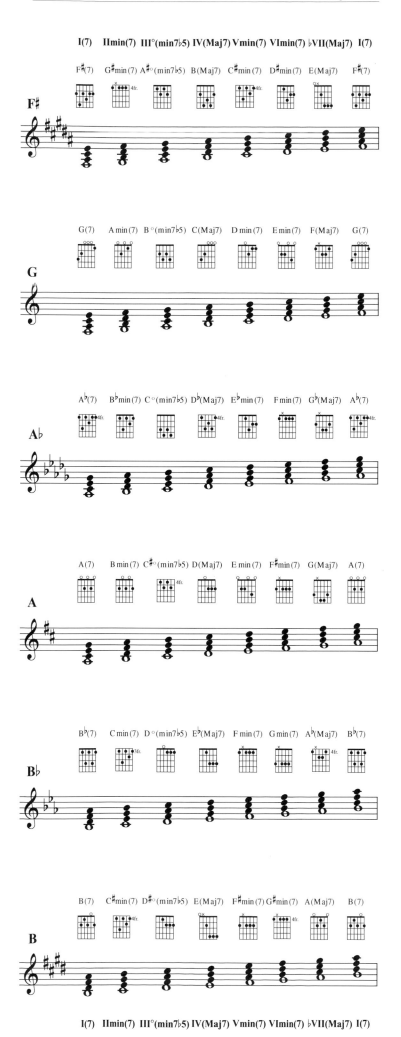

Mixolydian Progressions

These progressions are based on the *Mixolydian scale.* Mixolydian is like major, but with a flat-7. This note is a common chord root in Mixolydian power progressions.

I	♭VII
C	B♭

"Paperback Writer" [G Mixolydian],
"Manic Depression" [A Mixolydian],
"Fire" [D Mixolydian]
"Reelin' in the Years" [A Mixolydian],
"Only You Know and I Know" [E♭ Mixolydian],
"Tears of a Clown" [D♭ Mixolydian],
"Don't Stop 'til You Get Enough" [E Mixolydian],
"Norwegian Wood" [E Mixolydian],
"My Generation" [F Mixolydian],
"Centerfold" [G Mixolydian],
"Boogie Fever" [F Mixolydian],
"Hollywood Nights" [E Mixolydian]

I	♭VII	IV
C	B♭	F

"Shake Your Body Down to the Ground" [E♭Mixolydian],
"I Want a New Drug" [A Mixolydian],
"Ghostbusters" [B Mixolydian],
"Boogie On Reggae Woman" [A♭ Mixolydian],
"Gloria" [E Mixolydian], "Last Time" [E Mixolydian]

Dorian

Dorian Chords

Imin(7) IImin(7) ♭III(Maj7) IV(7) Vmin(7) VI°(min7♭5) ♭VII(Maj7) Imin(7)

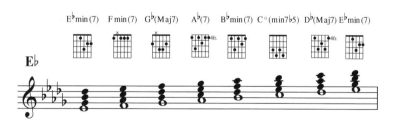

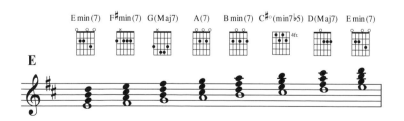

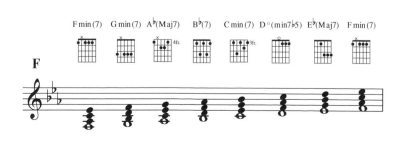

Imin(7) IImin(7) ♭III(Maj7) IV(7) Vmin(7) VI°(min7♭5) ♭VII(Maj7) Imin(7)

15

Imin(7) IImin(7) ♭III(Maj7) IV(7) Vmin(7) VI°(min7♭5) ♭VII(Maj7) Imin(7)

Dorian Progressions

The Dorian mode is like a natural-minor scale with a natural-6. Chords that contain the natural-6, such as the II and IV, are common in Dorian power progressions.

Imin	IV
Cmin	F

"Evil ways" [A Dorian], "I Wish" [E♭ Dorian], "Lowdown" [F Dorian], "Foxy Lady" [F♯ Dorian], "Owner of a Lonely Heart" [A Dorian], "Moondance" [A Dorian], "Billie Jean" [F♯ Dorian]

Imin	IImin	♭III	IImin
Cmin	Dmin	E♭	Dmin

"Billie Jean" [F♯ Dorian], "Moondance" [A Dorian]

17

Blues

Blues Chords

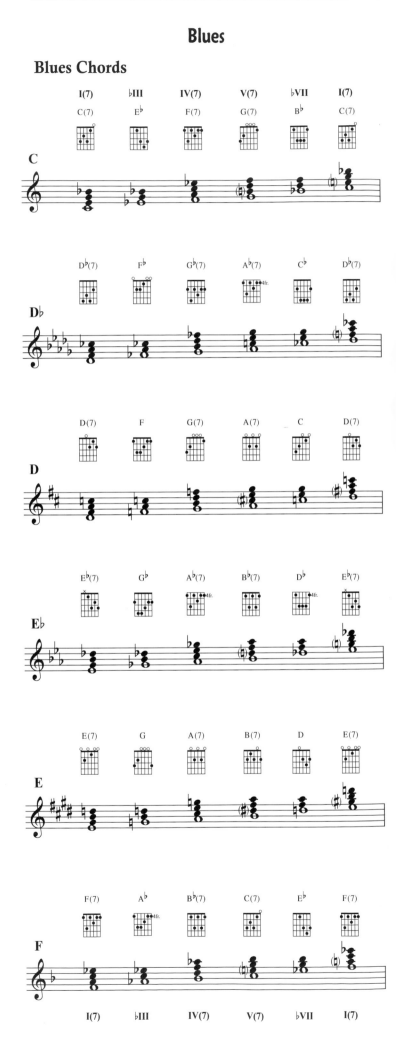

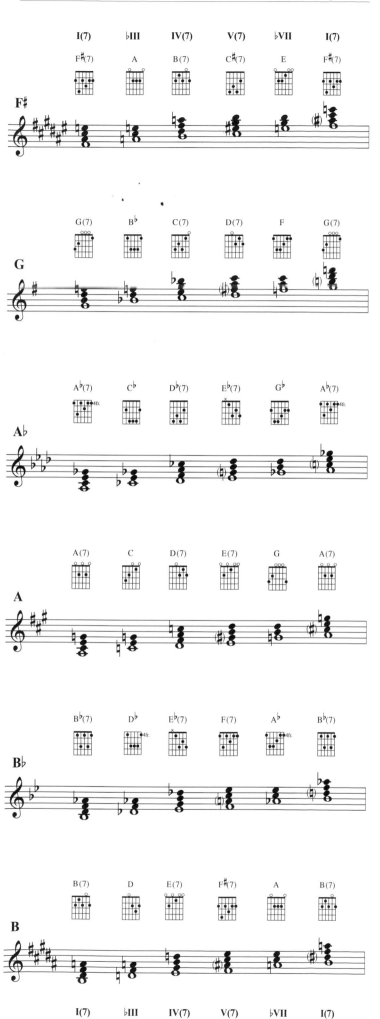

Blues Progressions

Blues harmonies are generally major or 7-chords based on roots from the minor pentatonic scale.

I7	IV7	
C7	F7	
I7	♭III	IV
C7	E♭	F

"Higher Ground" [E♭], "Purple Haze" [E], "I Can See for Miles" [E], "Born to Be Wild" [G]

12-Bar Blues

The most common blues progression is called the *12-bar blues.* It is twelve measures long, with the chords in this order.

I7	IV7	I7
IV7	I7	
V7	IV7	I7
C7	F7	C7
F7	C7	
G7	F7	C7

"Johnny B. Goode" [A], "Can't Buy Me Love" [C],
"Pink Cadillac" [E], "She's a Woman" [A],
"Dancin' in the Dark" [C],
"Still Haven't Found What I'm Looking For" [D],
"I Feel Good" [D], "Sunshine of Your Love" [D],
"Birthday" [A], "Boys" [E], "Day Tripper" [E],
"You Can't Do That" [C], "Change the World" [F],
"Gimme One Reason" [G], "Life in the Fast Lane" [E],
"Hey, Hey, Hey, Hey" [G]

2. Fifty-three Songwriting Ideas

Use these techniques to customize your progressions.

1. Change the groove. Try different tempos, rhythmic feels, rhythmic levels, and rhythmic ideas (motives).

2. Use different grooves in the verse, prechorus, chorus, bridge, or other sections. Make them contrast.

3. Create a song section out of the progressions. Repeat the progression exactly, with a chord variation, or with a change to the motive.

4. Add a note to any major chord. Try the 6, Maj7, Maj9, or add2.

5. Add a note to any minor chord. Try the 6, Min7, Min9, Min 11, or add2.

6. Add a note to any power chord. Try the add2.

7. Add a note to any seventh chord. Try the 9, 13, or ♯9.

8. Substitute a major chord's third with a sus2 or sus4.

9. Substitute a minor chord's third with a sus2 or sus4.

10. Substitute any seventh chord with a 7 with a 6, 7sus4, or 11.

11. Alternate versions of a chord within a progression. A "I7 IV7" (C7 F7) progression could become a "I I7 IV7" (C C7 F7) progression.

12. Substitute any chord of a power progression with a similar chord of a different type, borrowed from another key. For example, in major, try a IV7 (from blues) instead of a IVMaj7 (from major).

13. Substitute the root of any chord in a power progression with a root borrowed from another key. For example, in major, try a ♭III (from minor) as a root, rather than the usual natural-III (in major).

14. Build tension to the dominant by using the secondary dominant: the V of V, which is a major II chord in major. In the key of C, go from D major to G major to C (instead of the usual D minor to G major).

15. Create contrast between song sections. Whatever you do in one section, do something different in the next.

16. Use two different progressions in the same song section.

17. Use the same chord progression in two different song sections.

18. Use different chord progressions in different sections.

19. Use the same progression in the verse and chorus, but change it in the prechorus.

20. Change the overall length of the progression.

21. Change the duration of one or more chords in the progression.

22. Change the order of the chords.

23. Subtract a chord from the original progression.

24. Add a chord to the original progression.

25. Replace a chord in the original progression.

26. Add a repetitive melodic idea (a *pedal*) to the original progression.

27. Set your lyrics to chords that *parallel* their emotional content.

28. Set your lyrics to chords that *contrast* their emotional content.

29. Use a full cadence into the chorus, ending the verse on V7 (G7), and beginning the chorus on I (C).

30. Use a deceptive cadence into the chorus, ending the verse on V7 (G7) and beginning the chorus on a chord other than I. Try VImin (Amin) or IV (F).

31. Lead into the chorus using a half cadence, ending the verse on I (C) and beginning the chorus on V (G).

32. Make a title emotionally ambiguous by approaching it using a deceptive cadence (V to VImin, or G to Amin).

33. Set a refrain line to a plagal cadence (IV I, or F C).

34. Repeat any cadence to form a chorus.

35. Set the title only on a cadence.

36. Use a bridge that avoids the tonic chord.

37. Modulate to a *parallel* key. In C major, modulate to C minor.

38. Modulate to a *relative* key. In C major, modulate to A minor.

39. Modulate to an unrelated key, via a chord that exists in both keys.

40. Modulate within a verse.

41. Modulate to a new key at the chorus.

42. Begin your melody on a chord tones.

43. Begin your melody on a neighbor note to a chord tone.

44. Write melodic phrases that are the same length as your harmonic phrases.

45. Write melodic phrases that are *shorter* than your harmonic phrases.

46. Write melodic phrases that are *longer* than your harmonic phrases.

47. Move the bass in parallel motion with the melody. Voices move in the same direction, maintaining the same intervals.

48. Move the bass in similar motion with the melody. Voices move in the same direction, though sometimes by different intervals.

49. Move the bass in contrary motion to the melody. Voices move in opposite directions.

50. Move the bass in oblique motion to the melody. One voice stays the same, the other changes direction.

51. Use a different bass line in the verse and chorus.

52. Use the same bass line in the verse and chorus.

53. Base your song on a riff (repeating lick), usually in the guitar or bass.

3. Hit Song Forms

Songs may include any of the following types of sections.

Essential Sections

Nearly all songs have a verse and either a refrain or a chorus.

Verse	Verses tell the story. Generally, there is little repetition of lyrics within a verse. Lyrics change on each new verse. Verses may end in a refrain.
	These are the most common rhyme patterns for the verse lyrics. (An x means that the line doesn't rhyme.)

1.	a	b	a	b
2.	a	a	a	a
3.	x	a	x	a
4.	a	a	b	b

Refrain	The title or other lyric hook. The same, every time it appears. Though the rest of the verse lyrics may change, the refrain's lyrics generally remain the same.
Chorus	Arrival point of the song, generally telling the song's main idea, and often including the title. Often repetition of lyrics. Chorus lyrics tend to remain on each new chorus.
	These are the most common chorus structures used in hit songs. ("T" = Title, "–" = swing line)

1.	T	T		
2.	T	T	T	T
3.	T	–	T	–
4.	–	T	–	T
5.	T	–	–	T
6.	–	–	–	T
7.	T	–	–	–

24

Additional Song Sections

Many songs also include some or all of the following sections.

Intro	Beginning material. Sets up the song (usually leading into the first verse). May be unique material, but generally, it comes from somewhere else in the song, such as the verse's groove or the last few bars of the chorus.
Prechorus	Transitional material connecting the verse to the chorus. (Sometimes called a *transitional bridge.*)
Bridge	Song section that is generally different music from the primary sections. May include new lyrics and new music, with the characteristics of either a different verse or chorus. (Sometimes called a *primary bridge.*)
Instrumental Solo	A solo section can follow the form and harmonies of any other type of section. It can occur at any point of the song.
Outro	Ending material. Generally based on other material in the song, such as a repeated refrain or chorus (in whole or in part). It may consist of new material.

Common Hit Song Forms

Verse/Refrain
> "Got To Get You Into My Life," "Sounds of Silence," "The Times They Are a Changin'"

Verse/Refrain with a Bridge
> "I Feel Fine," "Just The Way You Are," "NY State of Mind"

Verse/Chorus
> "The Circle Game," "Tracks of My Tears," "Gone Country"

Verse/Prechorus/Chorus
> "If This Is It," "La Vida Loca," "How Will I Know"

12-Bar Blues
> "Pink Cadillac," "Can't Buy Me Love," "Money"

Common Arrangement Structure of an Entire Song

Intro (verse groove only)

Verse 1
> Prechorus
> Chorus

Verse 2
> Prechorus
> Chorus

Bridge

Verse 3
> Prechorus
> Chorus

Outro (chorus repeats and fades)

Common Song Running Time

Most hit songs have two or three different verses and last about three minutes.

4. The Songwriting Process

There are many ways to approach writing songs. Here is one process that you might try.

1. **Sketch the big picture.** You can modify this, throughout the process, but understanding the big picture helps keep ideas flowing.

   What is the style?
   What is the tempo?
   What is the groove?
   What are the riffs?
   What is the drum beat?
   What are the hooks?
   What is the overall lyric story?

   > **Sketch the Groove Early**
   >
   > A groove is both an engine for ideas and a sponge that holds everything together. It will develop as your song develops, and it will be a useful tool to you throughout the songwriting process.

2. **Write a section.** Take some ideas from the first step, and frame it into a section—a chorus, verse, or even a primary bridge. Include lyrics, if possible.

3. **Develop different section types.** Once you have developed a section, write the other song section types that will go with it. Generally, sections contain elements that make them contrast with each other, but also have a sense of continuity, so that they sound like different aspects of the same thing.

   > **Create Contrast**
   >
   > Examine the elements that went into making your first song section. Then do the opposite, for your next section. If you wrote a verse with lots of short notes in the melody, then write a chorus that has a lot of longer-duration notes. Change the chord rhythm, the phrase lengths, or any other aspects.

4. **Write subsequent sections.** Finish writing your lyrics for all verses, and look at your song as a whole.

5. **Add the intro, outro, bridges, and/or solo sections.** Think about the arrangement. How will you get from one section to the next? Make all transitions smooth.

6. **Develop how the song evolves over the entire arrangement.** What is the climactic point? How do you approach it and how do you leave it? Does the energy drop after the second chorus? Consider a bridge, or a modulation, or a change of instrumentation or texture.

7. **Practice and refine.** Once you have a completed song, sing it over and over. Look for spots that can be improved. Play it on your piano or guitar. Try different tempos or grooves. How does it feel to sing it?

> **Use Placeholders**
>
> If you find that you are spending too much time figuring out a detail of lyrics, melody, harmony, or groove, create a temporary placeholder, and move on. Fill in any words that rhyme, just to keep the lyric structure for the purposes of working on other parts of the song. Replace them when you can.
>
> Once you complete more of the song, the details will fall into place more easily.

5. Resources

1. **Register your copyrights.** Whenever you finish a song, download (or send away for) the appropriate registration forms from the U.S. Copyright Office.

   U.S. Copyright Office
   101 Independence Ave. S.E.
   Washington, D.C. 20559-6000
   (202) 707-3000
   www.loc.gov/copyright/

2. **Join a performance rights organization.** These organizations help make sure that you get paid royalties whenever one of your songs is performed, broadcast, or used on TV or in a film. The Harry Fox Agency helps to administer mechanical licenses.

   ASCAP
   One Lincoln Plaza
   New York, NY 10023
   212-621-6000
   www.ascap.com

   BMI
   320 West 57th Street
   New York, NY 10019-3790
   212-586-2000
   www.bmi.com

   The Harry Fox Agency
   711 Third Avenue
   New York, NY 10017
   212-370-5330
   www.harryfox.com

   SESAC
   55 Music Square East
   Nashville, TN 37203
   615-320-0055
   www.sesac.com

3. **Learn more about songwriting.** Take an online songwriting class or read any of the excellent songwriting books developed by Berklee College of Music.

   Berkleemusic.com/Berklee Press
   Berklee College of Music MS: 899
   1140 Boylston Street
   Boston, MA 02215
   www.berkleemusic.com

6. Authors' Bios

Jimmy Kachulis has trained thousands of songwriters, including Grammy award winning artists on A&M and MCA; staff writers at Almo Irving, Sony, Warner Brothers, and EMI; A&R people at Warner Brothers, BMG, and Sony; artists on independent labels; as well as independent songwriters. He currently teaches songwriting and lyric writing at Berklee College of Music and conducts songwriting clinics nationwide. Jimmy's songs have been recorded and broadcast internationally on Emmy Award winning TV shows *The Sopranos, Touched By An Angel, JAG, All My Children, The Young and the Restless, One Life to Live, The Jamie Foxx Show, Movie of the Week,* and various Showtime movies. He has written for Eric Gale, Stuff, and Martha Reeves. He has a BS from Hunter College CUNY and an MA in ethnomusicology from Tufts. He has authored the *Songwriter's Workshop* book series for Berklee Press, and created the *Songwriter's Workshop* on line classes for Berkleemusic.

Jonathan Feist has edited over fifty books about music, business, and technology, including the *Songwriter's Workshop, Berklee Instant,* and *Berklee Practice Method* series (to which he also co-authored the teacher's guide). He is Senior Writer/Editor of Berklee Press, the book-publishing division of Berklee College of Music, and teaches online courses in music through Berkleemusic.com. He holds bachelor's and master's degrees in composition from New England Conservatory.

Score Compose Arrange with
Berklee Press

Melody in Songwriting
Tools and Techniques for Writing Hit Songs

| ISBN: 0-634-00638-X | HL: 50449419 | BOOK | $19.95 |

By Jack Perricone

The Songwriter's Workshop: Harmony

| ISBN: 0-634-02661-5 | HL: 50449519 | BOOK/CD | $24.95 |

By Jimmy Kachulis

The Songwriter's Workshop: Melody

| ISBN: 0-634-02659-3 | HL: 50449518 | BOOK/CD | $24.95 |

By Jimmy Kachulis

Songwriting: Essential Guide to Rhyming
A Step-by-Step Guide to Better Rhyming and Lyrics

| ISBN: 0-7935-1181-X | HL: 50481583 | BOOK | $14.95 |

By Pat Pattison

Songwriting: Essential Guide to Lyric Form and Structure
Tools and Techniques for Writing Better Lyrics

| ISBN: 0-7935-1180-1 | HL: 50481582 | BOOK | $14.95 |

By Pat Pattison

The Songs of John Lennon: The Beatles Years

| ISBN: 0-634-01795-0 | HL: 50449504 | BOOK | $24.95 |

By John Stevens

Music Notation
Theory and Technique for Music Notation

| ISBN: 0-7935-0847-9 | HL: 50449399 | BOOK | $19.95 |

By Mark McGrain

Music Theory

| ISBN: 0-87639-046-7 | HL: 50448043 | BOOK | $24.95 |

By Paul Schmeling

Modern Jazz Voicings
Arranging for Small and Medium Ensembles

| ISBN: 0-634-01443-9 | HL: 50449485 | BOOK/CD | $24.95 |

By Ted Pease and Ken Pullig

Jazz Composition: Theory and Practice

| ISBN: 0-87639-001-7 | HL: 50448000 | BOOK/CD | $39.95 |

By Ted Pease

Arranging for Large Jazz Ensemble

| ISBN: 0-634-03656-4 | HL: 50449528 | BOOK/CD | $39.95 |

By Dick Lowell and Ken Pullig

Reharmonization Techniques

| ISBN: 0-634-01585-0 | HL: 50449496 | BOOK | $29.95 |

By Randy Felts

Finale®: An Easy Guide to Music Notation

| ISBN: 0-634-01666-0 | HL: 50449501 | BOOK/CD-ROM | $59.95 |

By Thomas Rudolph and Vincent Leonard, Jr.